ANIMAL MONSTERS

Fantasies and Facts of the Animal World

David Taylor

Lerner Publications Company
Minneapolis

All words printed in **bold** are explained in the glossary on page 46.

Front cover: The moray eel

First published in the U.S. in 1989 by Lerner Publications Company.

Copyright © 1987 by David Taylor.
Original edition published 1987 by Boxtree, Ltd. London,
England under the title DAVID TAYLOR'S ANIMAL MONSTERS:
MYTHS, LEGENDS, FANTASIES AND FACTS.

Library of Congress Cataloging-in-Publication Data

Taylor, David, 1934-
    Animal monsters: fantasies and facts of the animal world/David
Taylor.
        p.   cm.
    Originally published as: David Taylor's animal monsters. London:
Boxtree, 1987.
    Includes index.
    Summary: Recounts the legends associated with such monsters as the
unicorn, werewolf, dragon and mermaid, and describes real animals
which might account for the legends.
ISBN 0-8225-2176-8 (lib. bdg.)
    1. Monsters—Juvenile literature. 2. Animals—Miscellanea—
Juvenile literature. [1. Monsters. 2. Animals.] I. Title.
QL89.T35 1989
001.9'44—dc19   88-36777
                                                              CIP
                                                              AC

Manufactured in the United States of America

1 2 3 4 5 6 7 8 9 10 98 97 96 95 94 93 92 91 90 89

Contents

Arabian Nights encounters the fabled "island fish" on which unwary sailors made anchor and proceeded to cook dinner, arousing the fish and causing it to plunge to the ocean floor with ship, sailors, and all. The huge "kraken," often reported off the coasts of Norway and North America, was said to

embrace whole ships in its tentacles. Norse mythology tells of *Jörmundgandr*, a monster that encircled the earth at the sea's bottom and created great storms as it strove to bite its own tail. In Japanese legend, *Jish-in-uno*, an enormous codfish, is blamed for all earthquakes and tidal waves.

Stories of sea serpents have persisted into modern times. In 1860, the captain of the *British Banner*, William Taylor, reported an encounter with a fearsome monster. In 1872, a passenger on the *Silvery Wave* reported a sea creature with an enormous fan-shaped tail, large, glowing eyes, and a head shaped like a bull's that was surmounted by a horny crest. As recently as 1966, Chay Blyth and John Ridgeway, rowing across the Atlantic, reported seeing the "writhing, twisting shape of a great creature 35 or more feet long."

What truth might there be in such accounts? Well, there are some unusual creatures in the oceans, and most of us have never seen them or anything like them. Many of these creatures could have been mistaken for monsters. Some have thought that the Bible's Leviathan is really a crocodile. In fact, most of the descriptions of this beast better fit the whale.

Whales are the most majestic and highly specialized animals in the world. They are *not* fish, but warm-blooded, air-breathing mammals that suckle their young on milk. Biggest of all whales is the endangered *blue whale*, which can grow up to 90 feet (27.5 m) long and can weigh over 100 tons—a good deal more than the biggest dinosaur. The animal's tongue alone weighs over 3 tons. Blue whales belong to the "baleen" group of whales that filter food through horny combs, called baleen, in their mouths.

The *right whale*, also belonging to the baleen group, normally has massive pale lumps on its jaws and near its **blowhole**. These are caused by **parasites** living on the whale's skin. Right whales can be up to 60 feet (18 m) long. Basking with their knobby heads and long backs just poking out of the water, they do look like enormous, dark crocodiles.

The other main group of whales is made up of those with teeth, including the *sperm whale*, the *beluga whale*, and the *killer whale*. The sperm whale can dive almost 10,000 feet (3,000 m) and can stay under water for up to two hours. Killer whales have lots of big, ferocious-looking teeth, and can move at speeds of up to 40 miles per hour

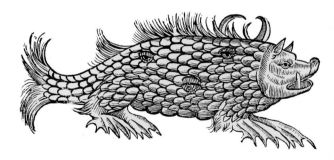

(64 kph). These tremendous animals might account for many sea monster sightings.

But some sea monster reports refer to a giant, snake-like animal—quite the opposite

This killer whale appears to be beached. At sea, it can stay under water for up to two hours.

of the barrel-bodied, neckless whale. Could a gigantic species of snake live in the ocean?

There are about 50 known species of sea snake. Apart from the *yellow-bellied sea snake*—one of the most widely distributed snakes in the world—all these species live in the warm, tropical waters of the Indian Ocean or the western Pacific. They usually prefer coastal waters and **estuaries,** but have sometimes been spotted as much as 140 miles (225 km) from land. Sea snakes have heavy, broad tails that are flattened on the sides like oars. Moving their bodies from side to side, they can swim rapidly through the water either backwards or forwards.

So, could the sea snake, which is known to float on the surface of the sea for long periods, have something to do with tales of monster sea serpents? Probably not. These pretty snakes are just too small. Most are under 5 feet (1.5 m) long and only rarely have sea snakes 10 feet (3 m) long been seen.

What about other kinds of snakes, big ones? Could they have taken to life beneath the ocean waves? Some of the biggest known snakes are very often found in and around water, although they live mainly on land. The *anaconda* and *reticulated python*, which often measure 30 feet (9 m) in length, are good swimmers. Pythons are regularly found along the waterfronts of Far Eastern cities such as Bangkok. Perhaps they have been mistaken for the sea monsters of legend.

The most fearsome animal known to live in the sea is truly "monstrous." It is the *great white shark*. Great whites have been known to attack anything—a person, a big whale, a boat, a metal cable. Usually, only

Parasites cause these strange bumps on the right whale's skin.

the dorsal fin is seen above the surface. But during an attack, this big fish sometimes thrusts its frightening head out of the water, exposing its cold stare, gaping mouth, and rows of wicked teeth.

The *whale shark* and the *basking shark* are even bigger than the great white. Both sharks can reach 43 feet (13 m) in length. Both are rare, harmless creatures, which feed by straining tiny organisms out of the water. Floating peaceably just below the surface, basking sharks are an impressive sight.

The great white shark rarely attacks people. It usually feeds on marine mammals such as whales.

Another member of the same group of non-bony fishes as sharks, is the giant *devil fish* or *manta*, one of the most sinister-looking and yet peaceable inhabitants of the seas. This strange, flat fish with a whip-like tail and "devil's horns" in front of its eyes can reach a size of more than 20 feet (6 m) across and can weigh over 1.5 tons. Like huge underwater bats, mantas "fly" through the sea and often swim or bask near the surface, with the tips of their fins or "wings" curling out above the water. Perhaps sea monster legends grew from descriptions of this strange creature.

Another fish we should bear in mind is the eel, which may have as much to do with sightings of sea serpents as with sightings of the Loch Ness monster.

The manta ray has two fins that project from its head like horns. This explains its common name, "devil fish."

Some sea monsters are not described as serpent-like at all. The *giant squid*, with its ten long arms used to capture and hold its prey, lives in the deepest abysses of the oceans. Specimens 60 feet (18 m) long and weighing around 2 tons have been recorded, and they may grow much bigger. Huge creatures of this type provide a convincing explanation of some sightings.

It is possible then to explain away some of the "evidence" for sea monsters. Certainly creatures we know nothing about, or can only guess at, are hidden in the ocean depths. Some may be the unexplained monsters of travelers' tales.

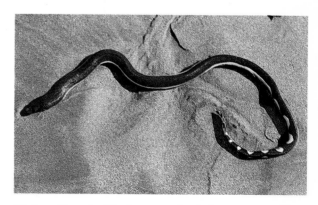

This yellow-bellied sea snake is just too small to be a "sea monster."

The Unicorn

The most beautiful legendary beast, and one that almost everyone could describe, (although no one has ever seen it), is the unicorn.

The earliest surviving description of a unicorn dates from around 400 B.C. Aristotle, the great philosopher, said there were two kinds of unicorn—the oryx and "the so-called Indian ass." Legends of the beast continue into modern times. Unicorns are frequently portrayed in **heraldry**. If you look at the British royal coat of arms you will see that a unicorn supports the right side of the shield, while a lion supports the left.

The unicorn also had a reputation for being very fierce, and anyone trying to capture one was told to be very careful. One trick recommended by unicorn hunters was to stand in front of a tree and to slip behind it when the beast charged. If the trick worked, the unicorn's horn would become stuck in the tree and the creature could then be captured.

The horn of the unicorn was said to have powers against poison. It was thought that if the horn was hollowed out, nobody could be poisoned by drinking from it. Until the French Revolution in 1789, vessels made of

"unicorn" horn were used in the French court to protect the king from poisoning. The horn was also highly valued as a medicine. It was sold by apothecaries (what we now call pharmacists) for more than 10 times the price of the same weight of gold. Until the nineteenth century, doctors carried bits of the horn, called "alicorn," which they ground down and used to treat all sorts of diseases.

So what really was "unicorn" horn? Sometimes, we know, the single-horned rhinoceros was confused with the unicorn. In the time of King Charles II of England, a cup made of "unicorn" horn was tested by London's Royal Society and found to be made of rhinoceros horn. But there are other creatures that are more likely to have given us the legend. A clue can be found in the report of the great sailor Sir Martin Frobisher, writing in 1577 after his second voyage in search of the Northwest Passage. In a bay northwest

of Labrador in Canada, he and his men found "a dead fish floating, which had in its nose a horn, straight and twisted, of length two yards lacking two inches, being broken in the top, where we might perceive it hollow, into which some sailors put . . . spiders. They [the spiders] presently died . . . by the virtue whereof we suppose it to be the sea unicorn." The "dead fish," in fact, was no fish at all, but a whale. It was one of the remarkable Arctic species that carries the single, long, twisted "horn of the unicorn": the narwhal.

It is this creature, the usual source of "alicorn," that gives us part of the unicorn legend. The other part is based on the oryx, and in particular the Arabian oryx, a species of antelope from one of the most desolate regions in the world.

Fake unicorns have been produced from time to time. But most likely the unicorn legend grew out of travelers' tales of the narwhal and the Arabian oryx, two real creatures that in many ways are as fantastic as the unicorn.

The *narwhal* is a very strange creature—the strangest of all the whales. It is a member of the group of toothed whales, and its Latin name, *Monodon monoceros*, means "one tooth, one horn." It actually has two teeth, but they are of no use for chewing things. The narwhal sucks its food. Narwhals are usually found in coastal waters of the Arctic Ocean. When fully grown, they are 13 to 16 feet (4 to 5 m) long and weigh 1,650 to 3,700 pounds (750 to 1,700 kg). Their coat is remarkable; it is made up of patches of black, cream, and grayish green. Male narwhals, and about two percent of females, have a single horn, which is actually the left tooth, enormously lengthened. It can be up to 10 feet (3 m) long, is twisted counterclockwise, and projects from the left upper lip downwards and towards the left. Nobody quite knows what the horn is for—perhaps it is just for display. It is sometimes

used as a lance in contests between males although the battles are not often serious.

Narwhals feed on fish, crustaceans such as shrimp, and mollusks such as squid. They live in herds. A herd is composed of groups of females with their young and bands of males, all of about the same size and horn length, which stick together like a troop of medieval knights. Females give birth after a pregnancy of some 15 months and suckle their young for 1.5 to 2 years. Herds probably stay together for life, and a narwhal may live for up to 40 years. There may be as many as 30,000 narwhals in existence. They are not endangered, although they are still sometimes hunted for their horn (as a collector's item, *not* as medicine).

The other creature that seems to have contributed to the unicorn legend is the *Arabian oryx*. The Arabian oryx is a specialist in survival in the most arid and sun-roasted places on earth. It is perhaps the most spectacularly beautiful of all the 24 species of grazing antelope.

Standing no more than about 3 feet (1 m) at the shoulder and weighing around 165 pounds (75 kg), the Arabian oryx isn't a very big creature. It has a bright white coat and brown legs. Its handsome head bears a chocolate-colored "**mask**" and two long, pointed horns that slope slightly backwards with light grooved rings around the lower

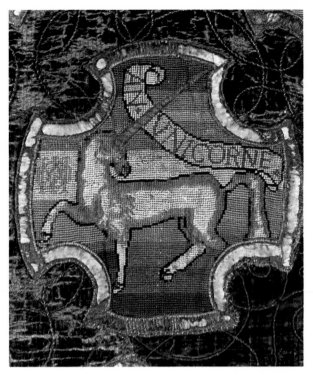

This velvet and canvas tapestry displays the legendary unicorn.

halves. Seen from the side, particularly from a distance in the shimmering glare of desert daylight, the Arabian oryx can appear to have but one horn. European travelers to Arabia in the early sixteenth century actually described the oryx as being the unicorn.

The oryx is built to survive in the desert. Its white coat reflects the sun's heat. But on a cold winter's morning the oryx can make the hairs of its coat stand on end for added warmth. The coat grows denser and its markings become darker in winter to absorb more heat at cooler times of day. Night and early mornings can be very cold in the desert, particularly between November and February. The oryx can survive with very little water, getting the liquid it needs from grasses, shrubs, and desert melons. To conserve water it passes very dry dung. A great wanderer, the oryx can travel many miles in a day—usually at a steady walk.

The horn of the narwhal is actually a long tooth. The narwhal has been called the "sea unicorn."

It has been known to cover 54 miles (90 km) in 18 hours. Its feet, which are broad and **splayed**, are ideal for walking on sand. In the summer, the Arabian oryx seeks shade early in the day, if necessary scraping out a shallow hole beneath a bush or in the side of a dune. It often digs a similar hole for sleeping at night.

Within an oryx herd, there is often serious fighting to establish who is in charge. A herd consists of about 14 animals, with equal numbers of males and females. The oryx has good vision and, if separated from its herd, it is able to follow tracks in the sand to locate other oryx. Female oryx give birth to a single calf after a pregnancy of 260 days, and most births occur between May and December. The newborn calf is a creamy fawn color and does not possess the distinctive markings of the adults.

Predators such as wolves and lynx pose

The Arabian oryx is an expert at survival in the desert. Its white coat reflects the fierce heat of the sun.

a threat to the oryx. Its other enemies are humans. When approaching a sick or wounded oryx, one must use great caution, for at such a time the animal is highly dangerous. It is not difficult to see where stories of the unicorn's fierceness came from!

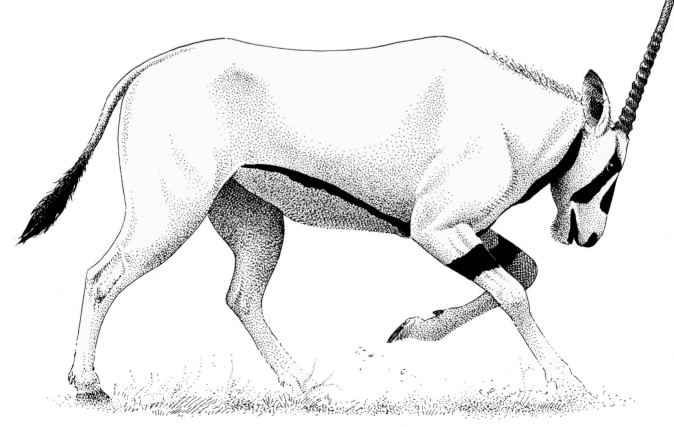

Seen from the side, the Arabian oryx appears to have only one horn.

The Werewolf

full moon on a winter's night is as clear and sharp as a diamond. You are in the mountains of Transylvania, in eastern Europe. A few miles out of the village, your car shudders to a halt. The house lights flicker in the village far below; the wind hisses softly. There is nothing to do, you decide, but to walk back and spend the night at the inn. A pity it's the night of the full moon. Of course, the pale light makes walking easier, but—in these parts there is a legend. The older folk in the village cross themselves and glance over their shoulders when they talk of it, for it is no legend to them. They believe that at full moon certain people are changed into wolves —*werewolves*. A dark figure watches you from behind a snow-covered pine tree. Is it a man? Suddenly it drops onto all fours. In the moonlight a hand stretches out against the snow. It is covered with hair and seems to have claws. The man, the creature, raises its head, bends it back, and as its teeth gleam coldly, lets out a piercing howl. . . .

The legend of the werewolf, the wolfman, goes back far into history. When witchcraft and magic were taken quite seriously, the changing of a human into a beast or the other way around seemed perfectly possible.

In 1598, in a wood in the west of France, a group of armed peasants found the naked corpse of a young boy, horribly mutilated

People have feared wolves for centuries. But in contrast to the legends, wolves rarely attack humans.

and covered in blood. As the peasants approached, they glimpsed what appeared to be two wolves running away into the trees. The men gave chase and, to their astonishment, found that they had caught not a wolf, but a man. His hands with their claw-like nails were dripping with fresh blood. The man turned out to be a beggar named Jacques Roulet and he was put on trial at Angers in August 1598. Roulet confessed before the judge. "I was a wolf," he said.

"Do your hands and feet become claws?"

"Yes, they do."

"Does your head become like that of a wolf?"

"I do not know how my head was at the time: I used my teeth."

Roulet was found guilty but, unusually for those times, was judged to be mentally ill and was sentenced to an asylum for a mere two years. In most such cases the "werewolf" was tortured, burned, or hanged.

Where did the widespread belief in werewolves come from? Wolves have always played a role in human culture, literature, and folklore. In primitive societies, hunters admired the speed, strength, and cunning of beasts of prey such as the leopard and the wolf. In ritual dances, they would mimic the behavior of such animals and dress in the skins of those animals. In some areas of the world, such rituals are still practiced.

Wolves are said to have raised small children. The Roman legend of the she-wolf suckling Romulus and Remus is quite well known. As late as the nineteenth century in India, there were several cases reported of children being reared by wolves.

The belief in werewolves may have been fostered by these stories, and by physical deformity in humans, such as strangely shaped noses or excessive hairiness. The legends about werewolves reflect what people have thought of and feared about wolves.

Few animals have been so unfairly treated. Far from being an evil hunter of humans, the wolf is a remarkable animal that deserves our attention and admiration.

Legend tells us that Romulus and Remus were nursed by a wolf. Stories of children raised by wolves continue into modern times.

Wolves are members of the dog family, which includes domestic dogs, wild dogs, jackals, coyotes, and foxes. The two species of modern wolves are the gray and the red. The red wolf is now thought to be extinct in the wild.

The *gray wolf* comes in over 20 different subspecies. It lives in a few forested areas of Europe, in the mountains of the Middle East, and in parts of Asia and North America. Once the most widespread of all mammals apart from humans, wolves have been steadily reduced in numbers by persecution and destruction of their **habitat**.

The gray wolf communicates by sounds and body language. A wolf's howl can be heard up to six miles away.

Wolves eat a variety of prey, from deer, moose, and caribou to beavers and hares. They have been known to eat almost every available type of small prey—small mammals, birds, snakes, lizards, fish, and even insects and earthworms. They eat carrion (the carcasses of dead animals), grass, and berries, and, when food is really scarce, wolves will scavenge for food scraps in garbage dumps. The type of prey or food tends to vary with the season.

The size of a wolf pack's territory depends upon how much food there is in the area, and can range from 40 to more than 400 square miles (100 to 1,000 sq km). Pack size also depends on food supply. When moose (heavy animals that can only be brought down by a large number of wolves working together) are plentiful, there may be up to 22 wolves in the pack, versus only 6 or 7 when the usual prey is deer.

Most wolf packs will stick to one territory all year round. In some areas of the northern **tundra,** when prey animals such as caribou migrate, the wolves move too. Nevertheless they return to their home ranges each summer to set up their dens. A particular pack marks its territory by howling and by **scent marking.** Howling can be heard up to 6 miles (10 km) away and advertises the presence of the pack, and scent is used especially along the boundaries of the territory. Wolves, like dogs, have a much better sense of smell than do human beings. They have 100 times as many receptors for detecting odors as people do. The territories of neighboring packs frequently overlap a little, but in such cases both packs tend to regard the area of overlap as a sort of "no-man's-land" and rarely visit it. Occasionally one pack will invade another's territory and take it over, if the resident pack can be defeated. Lone wolves, usually young animals that have left the family pack to find a mate and

set up a pack of their own, rarely scent mark or howl. They travel up to 20 times farther in their wanderings than does an established pack and try not to attract attention when in other wolves' territories.

Wolves mate for life as a rule and are ready to mate when they are two years old. Breeding occurs in late winter, and a litter of three to eight cubs is born in a den after a pregnancy of 63 days. At first the cubs are blind and helpless, but after four or five weeks they venture out of the den and are assisted by helpers in the pack who swallow food and then regurgitate it for the young. By the age of three to five months, the cubs are able to travel with the rest of the pack.

Like other members of the dog family, wolves communicate by body language and a variety of sounds—growls, yelps, howls, whines, and barks—each of which has a special meaning. An enormous variety of messages can be conveyed by the position of the wolf's ears and tail, the way its body is held, and its facial expression. In this way a wolf shows, for instance, whether it is aggressive, or whether it ranks higher or lower than another member of the same pack.

Are wolves dangerous to humans? Did they hunt and kill travelers in the past?

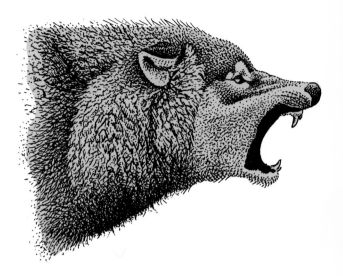

Very rarely. The reputation of the wolf as a killer is greatly exaggerated. Certainly, when they were common, wolves sometimes killed domestic animals, but not as many as has been claimed. As for reports of wolves killing human beings, many of these are pure fantasy.

Where dead hunters have been found partly eaten, with wolf tracks around them, it has been impossible to tell whether the person was attacked and killed by wolves, or died of something else and then was eaten as carrion. On the whole, stories of the wolf as a dangerous enemy of humans are as fantastic as stories of werewolves.

Wolves generally live in packs. Each pack marks its territory by howling and scent marking.

The Dogheaded Man

A person with a dog's head? Is this something from a horror film or a bad dream? In times gone by, people were quite sure that dog-people existed. The French physician Ambroise Paré described and sketched a "dogboy," who was born in 1493. The explorer Marco Polo said that people with dogs' heads lived on the Andaman Islands in the Indian Ocean.

The old fables and myths are full of creatures that are half human, half animal: werewolves, mermaids, and centaurs. The dogheaded man is but one of many combinations that, until the seventeenth century, and in some cases even more recently, were taken very seriously. Even as late as the 1890s, a distinguished British doctor wrote to a professional journal inquiring whether it was indeed possible for a woman to give birth to a dog. Of course, we know that such ideas are utter nonsense. But what lies behind them? Paré's "dogboy" and similar freaks were undoubtedly individuals afflicted with deformities or rare diseases that made them appear animal-like in some way. One of the most famous sufferers of this kind was the "Elephant Man," Joseph Merrick. Merrick suffered from the disfiguring disease, *neurofibromatosis* and was exhibited at freak shows in the late 1800s. Medical disorders causing excessive hair growth afflicted people such as Jo-Jo, the

The Egyptians worshipped Anubis, a god with the head of a jackal.

Although fantastic creatures such as these are obvious frauds, legends of dogheaded people persist. So we must look further for a possible answer. One source, perhaps, was the Egyptian god Anubis, depicted as a jackal-headed figure with a man's body. There are also a number of real creatures that could have suggested a dogheaded human. One of these is the *baboon*, a monkey that was once thought to be partly human. Indeed, in one description of baboons it was said that "their heads are like dogs and their other parts like man's"—but this writer also said that it was "the error of vulgar people to think that they are men."

Baboons do look more "human" than other monkeys, but it is their long, straight **muzzles** that give them some of the features of a long-nosed dog. Like humans, baboons walk with the whole of their foot placed on the ground. They can bring their thumbs across

dog-faced boy, whose face was said to be just like that of a Skye terrier. Adrien Jeftichew was a Russian peasant whose face, head, back, and limbs were covered with a brown hairy coat several inches long. He was called the "mandog" and had a son, Theodore, who was also hairy. Both were put on exhibition in Paris in 1875. Today, such people would be recognized as suffering from unusual physical disorders and be appropriately treated. Not so long ago, they were regarded as freak show attractions at fairgrounds and circuses.

Between the sixteenth and nineteenth centuries there was a craze for making sensational creatures. Bones and preserved portions of the bodies of various animals were made into instant **hybrids** with the aid of fine stitching and glue. Lots of "mermaids" were made that way and pulled in the crowds when they were put on show. "Dragons" and "sea monsters" were made from the dried corpses of fishes. *Furry* fish were made out of rabbit skin and parts of trout or salmon. A common trick in the western United States is to doctor a photograph to create a "jackalope," a giant jackrabbit with antlers.

Paré's "dogboy" was probably suffering from a medical disorder that could easily be treated today.

The long-haired gelada baboon lives in the highlands of Ethiopia and specializes in gathering grass seeds.

their hands to oppose the other fingers (and their big toes to oppose the other toes). They can travel long distances on foot and they spend less time in trees than do other monkeys. There are several species of baboon. By far the most handsome is the red and blue-faced *mandrill* that inhabits the forests of west central Africa. A long-haired baboon, the *gelada*, lives in Ethiopia and gathers seeds, roots, fruit, and insects. One of the

biggest species is the imposing *chacma baboon* of southern Africa. The one most like a human, however, is the *hamadryas* or *sacred baboon*, which was sacred to the ancient Egyptians. It is found in Africa from Somalia to the eastern Sudan, and in southern Saudi Arabia. The male hamadryas has a wonderful pink-red face with a long dog-like muzzle and a great cape of gray fur. Sitting on its rump in the sunshine with its hands often folded over its belly, it can indeed look like a little, rosy-cheeked, gray-haired gentleman—with a decidedly "doggy" face. Did travelers long ago bring stories about it back from Africa?

Another animal that we should consider is a species of *lemur*. Lemurs are found only on the island of Madagascar, off the east coast of Africa. They come in an amazing variety of types, from tiny *dwarf* and *mouse*

Male mandrills are more brightly colored than females, but all mandrills have the distinctive red and blue muzzle.

Ancient travelers probably never saw the orangutan, which lives only on the islands of Borneo and Sumatra.

lemurs weighing as little as 2 ounces (57 grams) up to big ones weighing over 15 pounds (7 kg). There was once a giant lemur the size of an orangutan, but looking more like a koala bear. It is one of at least 14 species of lemurs that have become extinct, largely because of human settlement on Madagascar.

The biggest of all surviving lemurs is the *indri*. It has a body up to 2.3 feet (70 cm) long that is shaped much like a human's. Unlike other lemurs, it has hardly any tail— just a stump a mere 2 inches (5 cm) long. The indri has large eyes and big, hairy ears shaped rather like ours. It possesses a dog-like snout. Its hands and feet are large, and its legs, like ours, are much longer than its arms. Its fur is thick but fine, partly black and partly white.

The indri lives in the **rain forest**, a habitat that is gradually shrinking under continued human exploitation. The animal feeds on leaves and fruit and is active during daylight hours, leaping from tree to tree and grabbing hold of trunks or branches with its body held upright. But an indri on the ground is more fun to watch. It has a unique way of

The male hamadryas baboon really does look like a little gray-haired man.

hopping along on both feet, with its arms held outstretched to the sides or above its head, and its body tilted backwards. Indris, like many humans, live in family groups made up of a mother, a father, and their offspring. Mothers carry the babies on their backs for up to the first six months of life. Another human-like feature of this lemur is its voice. One of its cries sounds just like that of a distressed child, and it also has a sort of howling song.

When Europeans first came across one of these creatures, their native guides shouted: "Indri! Indri!," meaning: "Look at that! Look at that!" The Europeans, not knowing any better, thought that "indri" was the name of the lemur. The native name for the indri is actually "babakoto." In the legends of Madagascar, the babakoto is described as being the ancestor of humans. In the way the indri sits and moves, and in some of the noises it makes, there are similarities to a human being. Its face resembles that of a friendly dog. Maybe travelers in times long past came across these animals and heard the legend of the babakoto, and then took home reports of a tribe of dogheaded people.

In the legends of Madagascar, the indri was the ancestor of humans.

29

The Abominable Snowman

Early in June 1977, Pang Gensheng, from Cuifeng in China, went to a gully to cut logs. He reported seeing a strange "hairy man," 7 or 8 feet (2 to 2.5 m) tall, who came close to him and made him think that he was going to have to fight for his life.

Was it the famous Abominable Snowman? Of all legendary monsters, he is perhaps the most intriguing to us human beings—for he may be our closest relative. Stories from many different parts of the world refer to a hairy creature that appears to be a cross between a large ape and a human being. In North America it is called *Sasquatch* or *Big Foot*. In Mongolia and the Caucasus Mountains, its name is the *Almas*. Most famous of all, in the Himalayas and China, it is known as the *Yeti* or the *Abominable Snowman*.

Stories of "wild men" go far back in time. The *satyrs* of Greek and Roman mythology —half man, half goat—may have their origin in memories of such strange beings.

Grizzly bears are found in the American West. Perhaps the Sasquatch is really a grizzly.

Two main types of what we call wild men are reported still to exist. There have been numerous sightings and casts have been made of giant footprints left in the snow and earth. The Sasquatch and the Yeti are described as much taller than adult humans. The Almas is said to be smaller than the average man.

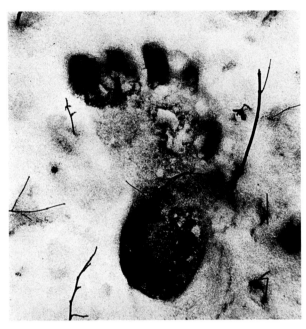

This footprint is too large to have been made by a human foot. Could it belong to the Yeti?

Most reports of the Sasquatch come from the heavily forested regions of western North America, from northern California to British Columbia. The Sasquatch is usually described as being 7 to 8 feet (2 to 2.5 m) tall. It is said to be heavily built and broad-shouldered with a short, strong neck. Its face is described as "monkey-like" or "ape-like" with a sloping forehead and pronounced eyebrow ridges. Its footprints are typically 14 to 17 inches (36 to 43 cm) long and about 7 inches (18 cm) wide. Reports say that the creature is furry or hairy and has dark skin. It walks like a person on two feet, though with a much longer stride. It is said that it can move very quickly and can also swim. A few of those who claim to have seen it say it makes sounds resembling those made by humans.

The Yeti of China and the Himalayas is described very similarly to the Sasquatch. Most sightings occur in the mountain forests, but it has also been sighted on the higher snow fields at altitudes of up to 20,000 feet (6,100 m). The Yeti is said to be taller than a human, with some estimates going up to 16 feet (5 m)! It is reported to have broad shoulders and long arms and to be covered in long hair that is usually described as brownish or reddish. Its face is ape-like, pale, and not very hairy. The Yeti is said to be solitary and **nocturnal**. Sometimes it is described as walking like a person on two legs, but it has also been seen moving on all fours. Its footprints resemble those of a barefoot man.

The Almas of Soviet Asia and Mongolia is reportedly much smaller than the Yeti at about 5.5 feet (1.7 m)—not quite as tall as an average adult man. It is said to be hairy, with a strong body and a more human-like face than the Yeti. Its jaws jut out, its chin recedes, and it has heavy eyebrow ridges. The Almas is said to make a few sounds, but it seems to have no language and is usually timid and unaggressive.

This "wild man" was captured on film in 1967. Some believe the film is a clever hoax.

No Sasquatch or Yeti has ever been captured. No sighting of a Sasquatch, Yeti, or Almas has ever been confirmed. The alleged footprints of the wild men have led to much debate among scientists. But most agree that the footprints *could* be made by a large **primate**.

Only once has a "wild man" been filmed. That was in October 1967, in Bluff Creek Valley, northern California, when some poor-quality movie film was shot of what was said to be a Sasquatch. Some specialists think the beast is something new to science, while others believe the film is a clever hoax.

So, could such creatures exist? Of course they could. All the wild men reports of modern times come from places that are desolate, often unexplored, and largely or completely uninhabited. Large numbers of unknown species could exist in these regions. It wasn't so long ago that scientists first discovered the giant panda, the coelacanth, the okapi, the pygmy chimpanzee, and the Komodo dragon. Every year many new animals are identified. What is more, there are too many reports of the Sasquatch and other "wild men" for us to dismiss them as pure imagination.

"Wild man" tracks resemble those made by a person walking on two feet. Bears can leave enormous prints, but they prefer to travel on all fours.

Could the Yeti be a gorilla?

But what sort of animal *known* to science might explain these sightings? It is perfectly possible that mistakes have been made. *Bears*, for example, which are hairy and as big as, or bigger than humans, are found in both Sasquatch and Yeti territory. The footprint of a large bear can, under certain conditions, resemble that of an enormous man. Bears can walk upright on their hind legs, though they do so awkwardly and only for short periods.

Could some sort of primate, an ape or a monkey, be the answer? No primates other than humans are known to live in North America. In the Himalayas and China, however, there are a few possible candidates. The *hanuman* or *common langur* has sometimes been mistaken for a Yeti. It is gray or gray-brown in color and has been seen at altitudes of up to 13,200 feet (4,000 m). It can stand upright or "dance" along on its feet, but only for brief periods. Langur footprints can look like a human's, but are much smaller than those thought to belong to the Yeti.

The *mountain gorilla* is found at altitudes of between 5,300 and 12,500 feet (1,600 and 3,800 m), whereas the Yeti has normally

The smallest of the great apes, the chimpanzee is just too little to fit the "wild man" description.

been sighted at higher altitudes. But, no known gorilla could explain the Yeti, since gorillas only live in the tropical forests of central Africa. *Orangutans* are only found in Borneo and Sumatra so these could not account for sightings of the creature. But it is just possible that some gorilla-like great ape is hidden away in unexplored regions of the Himalayas or western North America.

But the latest theories proposed to explain the Sasquatch, Yeti, and Almas involve much more sensational primates. It has been suggested that descriptions of the Sasquatch and the Yeti fit well with what we know of a great ape called *Gigantopithecus*. Gigantopithecus, however, is thought to have become extinct over a half million years ago. Perhaps the Yeti and the Sasquatch are descendants of this same animal?

The Almas seems to be something different. According to recent theories it might be a descendant of the *Neanderthal* people, whom we closely resemble. The Neanderthals lived in Europe, Asia, and Africa 125,000 to 35,000 years ago. From examining fossils,

we know they had long, wide heads set on thick necks. Their eyebrow ridges were massive and their chins were small. This fits descriptions of the Almas.

Perhaps the Almas, if it exists, is a descendant of the Neanderthals. The Yeti too might be descended from some great ape, if not actually a Gigantopithecus. As for the Sasquatch—it remains a mystery.

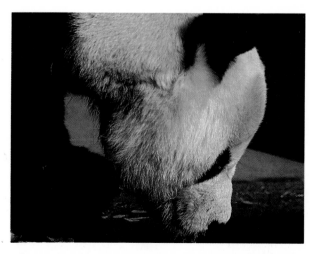

The giant panda wasn't discovered until 1869. It is possible that some large animal species have yet to be discovered.

33

The Vampire

attered clouds brush the face of the full moon. In a darkened bedroom, the sleeper is unaware of an owl hooting and a clock chiming midnight. A shadow moves. Soundlessly, it brings forth a cloaked figure. A shaft of moonlight briefly lights up a deathly pale face, The creature's lips part to reveal sharp fangs. Its gaze falls upon the sleeper's throat. Dracula, prince of vampires, goes in search of a meal of blood!

Whew! Late night horror films can still send a chill down your spine. But it's all good fun, and nothing more than fantasy. After all, Dracula doesn't exist, does he? Creatures that suck blood from unsuspecting victims aren't real, are they?

In 1732, a vampire that was said to have appeared in Belgrade, Yugoslavia, was described thus: "It leaned to one side, the skin was fresh and ruddy, the nails grown long and evilly crooked, the mouth slobbered with blood from its last night's repast.

Accordingly a stake was driven through the chest of the vampire, who uttered a terrible screech whilst blood poured in quantities from the wound. Then it was burned to ashes." Vampire stories are to be found in the traditions of every nation and there really *was* a Dracula. He was a very cruel king, Vlad Tepes, who ruled part of Romania in the fifteenth century. He signed his name "Vlad Dracula," which means "son of the dragon." His bloody reputation, however, was owing to his brutal methods of torturing and killing enemies. His own people considered him a hero because of his success in fighting the Turks.

Dracula is a favorite with movie-goers.

So if the real Dracula didn't drink blood, where does the legend come from? First let us look at the vampire legends in more detail. Basically, the belief was that corpses could rise from their coffins at night to suck the blood of the living, making new vampires of their victims, and return to the grave before daybreak. A French Benedictine monk, an expert on vampires, wrote in 1746, "we are told that dead men ... return from their tombs, are heard to speak, walk about, injure both men and animals whose blood they drain ... making them sick and finally causing their death. Nor can the men deliver themselves unless they dig the corpses up and drive a sharp stake through these bodies, cut off their heads, tear out the hearts, or else burn the bodies to ashes." Legends about vampires seem to have appeared in Romania and Hungary at the beginning of the sixteenth century. The novel *Dracula*, published in 1897 by an Englishman, Bram Stoker, did more than anything else to spread the legend.

Recently, it has been suggested that there could be a connection between vampirism and a very rare blood disease called *porphyria*. Patients suffering from this complaint develop severe anemia (shortage of red blood cells) and so are very pale. Their teeth wear away and become pointed, their skin becomes allergic to light, and their behavior changes. Put all these symptoms together—pale face, pointed teeth, an aversion to light, and unusual behavior—and you have a good description of the traditional vampire. Modern medicine can treat such cases very effectively. In the past, however, the condition would have proved fatal. But—here is the twist—in days gone by, anyone suffering from this disease would have felt much better if he or she had drunk some fresh blood!

But that is not the whole story. Vampires—creatures who depend completely on a diet of blood to stay alive—do exist. These creatures probably have something to do

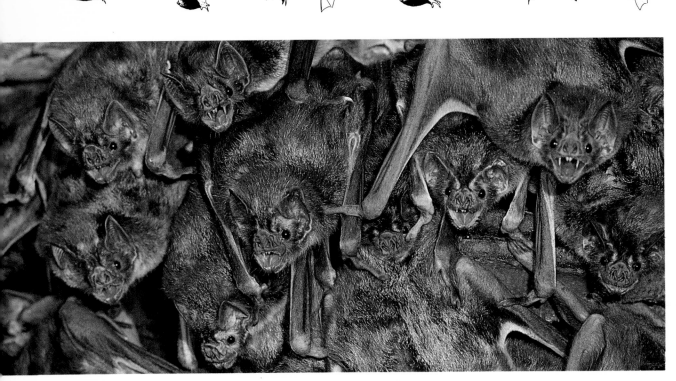

Vampire bats live in colonies of up to 100 animals. Like most bats, they sleep during the day and fly at night.

with the vampire myths. There are parasitic worms, leeches, and some insects that are specialist bloodsuckers. But there is one blood-feeding mammal that might have come straight out of a horror film—the *vampire bat*.

The vampire bat, a bizarre creature, is the only dangerous bat among the 951 different species of bat in the world. It lives in South and Central America. There are three species of vampire bat: two rare ones that feed mainly on the blood of birds, and the *common vampire bat*, which prefers to attack cattle, horses, pigs, and occasionally human beings. The vampire is brown in color, although the rare *white-winged vampire*, has white tips and edges on its wings. Vampires are average-sized bats, weighing between .5 and 1.5 ounces (14 and 43 gm) and are 2.5 to 3.5 inches (6 to 9 cm) long. The common vampire bat has 22 teeth, the front 10 of which are sharp and pointed. Particularly noticeable are the two upper center teeth or *incisors*. They glint like white daggers whenever the bat grimaces, as it frequently does.

A vampire bat will feed for up to 20 minutes on its victim. In one year, it can consume over 5 gallons (19 liters) of blood. The blood-loss can weaken the victims and reduce their resistance to disease. Far more important, vampire bats can actually *kill* by transmitting the deadly rabies virus in their saliva. Over one million cattle and about 30 people die each year in South America from rabies carried by these nocturnal mammals.

A vampire bat out hunting behaves very much like the monster of legend. It prefers moonless nights, when it is less likely to be pounced upon by its enemy, the owl. Unlike some bats, it has excellent eyesight, and it uses this and its sense of smell to locate its prey. Often it lands on the ground near the victim and then hops and leaps onto it. It holds its wings out like a cloak and bares its two upper teeth in its open mouth—just like Dracula!

The vampire bat doesn't actually *suck* blood, but laps it up from a wound painlessly inflicted in its victim by its two incisors.

Vampire bats are only a few inches long. This photo of a bat feeding on a chicken in Trinidad is greatly enlarged.

These teeth are as sharp as a surgeon's knife, and the wound they inflict is a groove .1 inch (2.5 millimeters) long. A special chemical in the bat's saliva stops blood from clotting, so that it will continue to flow. Two long grooves in the bat's tongue expand during feeding and help to draw up the liquid.

Vampire bats live in colonies of up to 100 animals. They sleep throughout the day and become active during the darkest period of the night. They like to fly along riverbeds and rarely venture more than 1.2 miles (2 km) away from one of these corridors. Bats are fussy in choosing their victims. They prefer certain breeds of cattle, and they select cows over bulls and calves over adults. Common vampire bats used to feed on wild animals, but they have adapted to preying upon **domesticated** species over the past 400 years. Vampire bats are rarely seen in zoos. If a zoo were to add some vampire bats to its collection, it would have to keep them under permanent **quarantine** conditions to prevent the spread of rabies.

As for "human" vampires, there is no need to be afraid that Dracula will pay you a

The bat inflicts a wound with two sharp incisors. A chemical in the bat's saliva stops its victim's blood from clotting.

visit in the dead of night. Yet the belief in such creatures persists. In 1973 in Stoke on Trent, England, a man, terrified of vampires, locked himself in his room and placed salt and garlic—traditional vampire repellents—all around him on his bed. He even slept with a clove of garlic in his mouth and choked on it and died. Truly, this poor fellow was a real victim of vampires!

The Dragon

There's one monster that has had a lot of publicity down through the ages. The dragon roars and rampages through the legends and traditions of many of the world's oldest cultures. Though often associated with evil and darkness, the dragon is occasionally a symbol of good fortune and wisdom. The Roman cohort (a division of soldiers) used the dragon as its emblem.

Viking warriors painted dragons on their shields and carved dragons' heads on the prows of their ships.

Before the Norman invasion of 1066, the dragon was the principal battle emblem of Anglo-Saxon rulers in England. The dragon is also associated with Wales and appears on the Welsh flag. In the Far East, the dragon was a symbol of wealth and good luck. For centuries it was the national symbol of China and the emblem of the Chinese emperors.

On what was the widespread belief in the power of dragons based? In times past, dragons weren't regarded as fanciful creations of the imagination, but as real creatures. Why should so many different peoples have believed in dragons if there were not animals in some ways like them?

The word "dragon" comes from the Greek *drakon*, meaning "sharp-sighted." The word came to refer to snakes, particularly big

snakes. Originally the dragon was a fabulous snake.

Ancient civilizations knew about and respected snakes, particularly the big ones. Most big snakes, terrifying as they may appear, are *not* **venomous** and are not usually dangerous to human beings. The biggest and heaviest of all snakes in the Western Hemisphere is the *anaconda*, which is known to reach lengths of about 30 feet (9 m). The *pythons* and *boa constrictors* reach lengths of 33 feet (10 m). All three belong to the family of constrictors, snakes that coil themselves around their victims and kill them by biting, swallowing, and suffocating them. A large specimen in its natural habitat, particularly when it is on the attack, is an impressive sight.

But where do the legs and wings of the legendary dragon originate? Well, ancestors of snakes once had legs long ago. Even today in some snakes you can find the **remnants** of hind legs in the form of little bones within the body and two small claws on the outside of the belly. There are other animals with legs that could also have contributed something to legends of dragons.

The dragon was frequently the symbol of warriors. Vikings carved dragon heads like this one on the prows of their ships.

One beast that in many ways recalls the legendary dragon is the *crocodile*. It has legs, of course, and it likes to bask on land in the heat of the day with its mouth wide open, to get rid of excess heat. This might have something to do with tales of the dragon breathing fire.

Crocodiles and their close relatives look like dragons and are in many ways awesome beasts. There are 23 species of crocodilians— including crocodiles, caimans, alligators, and gavials. One of the biggest is the *estuarine* or *saltwater crocodile* of India, southern China, Malaysia, Australia, New Guinea, and the Philippines. Fully grown saltwater males average 15 feet (4.6 m) in length and weigh around 1,100 pounds (500 kg). All other crocodilians live in fresh water. Some crocodiles, especially saltwater crocodiles, will attack and eat humans.

Crocodiles are powerful swimmers. They fold their limbs against their bodies and push themselves along with strokes of their muscular tails. On land, crocodiles can run quite fast, keeping their bodies well off the

In China, the dragon was a symbol of good luck. People believed it would prevent evil spirits from spoiling the new year.

39

This anaconda of the Brazilian jungle kills by coiling itself around its victim.

ground. Male and female crocodiles find one another by sound and smell. During the mating season, the males emit a loud bellowing noise that can be heard over a long distance. Crocodiles reproduce by means of eggs, which are white, oval, covered with a thick, chalky shell, and laid on land. The number of eggs may vary from 20 to 90 according to the size of the crocodile. The site and type of nest vary. The *Nile crocodile* deposits its eggs in the sand, in a hole 18 to 25 inches (46 to 64 cm) deep. It arranges its eggs in two layers with a layer of sand between. Most other species sweep together a mound of vegetable **compost** and deposit the eggs in the center of this pile. In this "compost heap," the heat of the rotting vegetable matter, as well as sunshine, **incubates** the egg. The mother crocodile remains near the nest, visiting it from time to time and, warned by the hiccup-like cries that the young produce when ready to leave the egg, scratches away the covering of the nest and leads her brood to the water. The young crocodiles break their way through the strong eggshell with an "egg tooth" on the tip of the snout. The tooth is lost soon after hatching. As soon as the little crocodiles are out of the egg they are able to look after themselves. They grow fairly rapidly for the first few years—usually about 1 foot (30.5 cm) per year under good conditions—and then slow down.

But what about two living reptiles that are actually *called* "dragons?" One of these has the Latin name *Draco volans*, which means "flying dragon," and like the legendary dragon it can take to the air! The flying dragon is a lizard found in the East Indies

A Nile crocodile basks with its mouth open to get rid of excess heat.

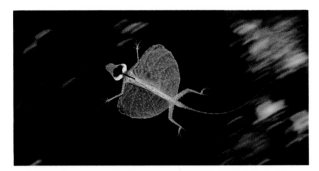

A "flying dragon" glides through the air in the forests of southeast Asia.

and southern Asia that possesses wing-like folds of skin on each side of the body. These are supported by greatly elongated ribs. When spread, these "wings" allow the lizard to glide through the air as it leaps from tree to tree. However, the folds cannot be flapped like a bird's wings to give the power of flight.

The other reptile known as a dragon is much bigger. In fact it is the biggest lizard in the world, and yet it was not discovered by scientists until the 20th century. It is the *Komodo dragon.*

From the beginning of this century, there were reports of giant lizards living on one or two small islands in Indonesia. Then, in 1912, a pilot of a light plane made a forced landing on the island of Komodo and

The Komodo dragon wasn't discovered until 1912. The International Society for Cryptozoology believes that other strange animals have yet to be found.

actually saw one. It was, he reported, just like a dragon. Soon after, an expedition was formed to hunt for some of the creatures, and four specimens, each over 10 feet (3 m) long, were captured. The Komodo dragon belongs to a family of large lizards called "monitors," of which there are about 30 species, in Africa, the Middle East, southern Asia, and Australia.

The Komodo dragon is an impressive, powerful creature. No one knows why it is only to be found on three tiny islands in Indonesia. It possesses a dark gray green skin of small knobby scales. Like many lizards, it shoots its long yellow-pink tongue in and out from between its jaws. Could the lizard's flickering tongue be the dragon's "flame?"

Komodo dragons can kill pigs and small deer. A dragon once brought down a 1,300-pound water buffalo.

Flying Monsters

The "roc," in the story of "Sinbad the Sailor," is a fabulous white bird of enormous size and such strength that it could "truss elephants in its talons" and carry them to its mountain nest. Monster birds that were capable of preying on humans and large animals are found, like stories of other legendary beasts, in the folk traditions of many countries. Could a large bird, living or extinct, ever have been capable of doing such a thing?

The heaviest living bird of prey is the *Andean condor* of South America. It can weigh up to 24 pounds (11 kg). The heaviest eagle, the *harpy eagle*, also of South America, can weight over 20 pounds (9 kg). The Andean condor has the largest wings of any bird, and with wings outstretched measures almost 10 feet (3 m) across. The harpy eagle hunts close to the ground and has relatively short, but very broad wings that are about 6.5 feet (2 m) across. Although condors and eagles are extremely powerful birds that can *kill* prey weighing much more than themselves, they cannot *lift* a weight greater than that of their own body.

The largest flying animal that ever existed was probably *pteranodon*, a winged reptile,

People used to believe that barnacle geese hatched from trees growing along the seashore.

believed to have lived around 100 million years ago. This **carnivorous** beast had a wing-span of 18 feet (5.5 m). Despite its great size, it was extremely light. It had hollow bones with walls as thin as a playing card, so it is unlikely that even a pteranodon could have carried anything very heavy.

It seems, then, that the roc and its kind are imaginary animals based on what people know of the habits of birds of prey. Birds bigger than condors and eagles do exist, of course. But the *ostrich*, the *cassowary*, the *emu*, and the *rhea* are all unable to fly. The *elephant bird* was a giant bird that once

The Andean condor weighs up to 24 pounds. It can kill animals that weigh much more than itself, but cannot lift them.

lived on Madagascar. It was still there when the French occupied parts of the island in the second half of the seventeenth century. It is likely that this bird, named *Aepyornis*, lived on the island until about 200 years ago. It was much bigger than an ostrich, standing 10 feet (3 m) high, and it had legs as thick as those of a young elephant. Pieces of its eggs can still be found in southern Madagascar. The eggs could indeed have held a gallon of water, for they measured 13 by 9.5 inches (33 by 24 cm), with a shell .25 inches (6 mm) thick. Aepyornis eggs are the biggest bird eggs that have ever been discovered.

The phoenix rises from the ashes of its funeral pyre.

The mythical barnacle tree

Another, even bigger flightless bird once lived in New Zealand. It was called the *moa* and there were several species of various sizes. The smallest moa was the size of a turkey. The largest was an ostrich-like monster 12 feet (3.7 m) high. Sadly, the bird is now extinct. The moa had no wings at all, unlike the ostrich, which possesses small ones. It had very strong legs and four toes. It seems to have been an **herbivore.**

Now, what would you say if someone told you that birds *grew out of trees*? You would probably say that the person was crazy. Yet that is exactly what many people used to believe. There were two versions of the legend. In the first story, the fruit of trees growing by the sea fell in the water and turned into geese. In the second story, a sticky substance from old ship's timbers developed into **barnacles** or, it was thought, *barnacle geese.*

These beliefs go back a long way, and it is from them that the barnacle goose gets its name. Barnacle geese are winter visitors to the British Isles. In earlier times, when it was unknown that they nested in the Arctic, it was assumed that the birds hatched from the shell-like fruit of a tree growing on the seashore. The "tree" was actually a type of barnacle that can look somewhat like a plant. The *goose barnacle (Lepas anatifera)* is an animal common in all seas and is often found attached to timber on the shore or the bottoms of ships. Basically, it is a shell on a stalk. It does look a bit like a goose's long neck and head. The goose barnacle is actually a crustacean, a relative of crabs and lobsters.

The most famous of all legendary birds is the *phoenix*. It is the bird said to rise from the ashes of its funeral pyre, and is a symbol of resurrection. All the ancient writers agreed that only one phoenix, a male, was alive at any one time. At the end of its life, usually said to last 500 years, it built a nest of spices and died in it. From its remains arose a young phoenix.

Real birds as spectacular as the mythical phoenix are the *birds of paradise*. According to legend, birds of paradise had neither wings nor feet, but passed their entire lives floating in the air, occasionally hanging from the branches of tall trees by their long tail feathers. Some people believed that these birds came directly from heaven, and for a long time they were called "birds of God."

Indeed, the real birds of paradise, of which there are 43 species, are probably the most spectacular birds in the world. The males have particularly elaborate and brilliantly colored **plumage**. Some have wire-like adornments among their tail feathers—which are *not* used for hanging from branches. Perhaps the most striking of all is the *blue bird of paradise*.

The condor, the bird of paradise, and the extinct elephant bird are awe-inspiring creatures. Certainly, when ancient people encountered these spectacular birds they were struck by their beauty and power. It is no wonder that they devised tales and legends to make these birds seem even more powerful and magical. Fortunately, the real birds have not disappointed us.

A Raggiana bird of paradise shows its spectacular plumage. Some people believed that these birds came from heaven.

Glossary

appendage A limb of an animal such as an arm, a leg, or a wing

barnacle A crustacean affixed to an object in the sea such as a rock, a ship, or a whale
blowhole A nostril in the top of the head of a whale

carnivorous Meat-eating
cold-blooded Having a body temperature consistent with the temperature of the environment; unable to generate its own heat
compost Decaying vegetable matter

domesticated Tamed; adapted to living and breeding near humans
dorsal Situated on the back of an animal

estuary An arm of the sea where it meets a river
extinct No longer in existence

habitat A natural home for an animal
heraldry A system of emblems and decorations used by families, nations, and armies
herbivore A plant-eating animal
hybrid The offspring of animals of two different breeds or species

incubate To provide warmth that causes eggs to hatch

mammal A warm-blooded animal with hair that feeds its young with milk
mask The face of an animal
mirage An optical effect in which distant objects may appear distorted
muzzle The projecting jaw and nose of an animal; the snout

nocturnal Active at night

parasite An animal that obtains food or assistance from another animal without making a useful contribution in return
plumage The feathers of a bird
predator An animal that kills and eats other animals
primate A member of the group of mammals that includes humans, apes, monkeys, and lemurs

quarantine Enforced isolation to prevent the spread of disease

rain forest A tropical forest receiving over 100 inches of rain per year
remnant A small, remaining trace

scent marking Using urine or other substances to mark territory
splayed Flattened and spread out
stag A male deer
suckle To give milk from the breast or udder

tundra A treeless plain in arctic and subarctic regions

ultrasonic Beyond the range of the human ear

venomous Having a poison-producing gland and able to inflict a poisoned wound

warm-blooded Having a constant body temperature regardless of the temperature of the surroundings; able to generate its own heat

Index

Acknowledgments

Illustrations and photographs are reproduced through the courtesy of Mary Evans Picture Library, pp. 7, 23, 31/Bruce Coleman Limited: pp. 7, 16 (J. Foott), 13 (J. Burton), 16 (J. and D. Bartlett), 17 (P. Ward), 21 (H. Jungius), 24 (G. Laycock), 28, 41 (A. Compost), 28, 29, 33 (B. Coleman), 28, 32 (R. Williams), 29 (H. Diller), 32 (E. and P. Bauer), 36, 43, (G. Ziesler), 41 (Mackinnon), 43 (A. Davies)/Seaphot Limited: pp. 8 (B. Merdsoy), 9 (R. Wood), 12 (C. Roessler), 17 (A. Giddings), 17 (K. Amsler), 33 (M. Yamamoto), 40 (R. Matthews), 40 (N. Greaves)/Fortean Archive: pp. 11 (A. Shiels, Hugh Gray), 19, 20, 23, 30, 31 (Rene Dahinden), 44/Aquarius: p. 35/Ardea: pp. 37 (A. Warren), 45 (E. Lindgren), 45 (D. Hadden)/ Bridgeman Art Library: p. 20. Front cover: Marty Snyderman. Other illustrations: David Quinn.

David Taylor is a veterinarian who works with wild animals around the world. From the Komodo dragon to the giant panda, from killer whales to gorillas, Taylor specializes in the problems that can beset the rare, the exotic, and the endangered.

His adventures have been recounted in his autobiographical series of *Zoovet* books and in the popular television series, "One by One," which has been shown in Great Britain, the United States, and many other countries. David Taylor has recently retraced Hannibal's epic journey across the Alps—with elephants—and has been involved in the rescue of two dolphins stranded in Egypt.